Tarot for Manifestation

Use the Cards to Make Your Desires a Reality!

James Wells

Tarot for Manifestation

Published by
Tarot Media Company
a Cigno E Gallo, Inc. company
58 West Portal Avenue, Suite 236
San Francisco, CA 94127-1304 USA
www.TarotMediaCompany.com

Tarot for Manifestation: Use the Cards to Make Your Desires a Reality / James P. Wells

Printed in U.S.A.

ISBN 978-0-9833024-3-8

Design by Rydell Downward • www.QWerks.com

The Gaian Tarot image on the front cover appears by kind permission of Joanna Powell Colbert.

Images from The Shining Tribe Tarot are used with the gracious consent of Rachel Pollack.

Cards from The Medicine Woman Tarot are included with appreciation to Carol Bridges.

The William Blake Tarot of the Creative Imagination images are available with the generous permission of Ed Buryn.

Images from the Motherpeace Tarot appear with with the gentle consideration of Motherpeace, a pseudonym for Vicki Noble & Karen Vogel, 1981.

Acknowledgements

Thank you to Gail Fairfield, Mary Greer, Rachel Pollack, and James Wanless for their beautiful demonstrations of what tarot can be.

Thank you to the Goddess in Her form as Brigid, whose flame fuelled me and whose waters calmed me.

Thank you to Joanna Powell Colbert for permission to use the image of the Nine of Water from the Gaian Tarot as the cover art. You can see more wonderful cards at www.gaiantarot.com

Thank you to Anastasia Haysler and Tarot Media Company for bringing Tarot for Manifestation back to life.

Thank you to Cyrus Shirkool for generous computer time and for the author photo in the back of the book.

Thank you to the wonderful people who come to me for consultations, workshops, and classes. Your willingness to explore is exquisite! A special bow of gratitude goes to those who allowed me to use their examples in this book.

Thank you to the tarot, my primary soul language and teacher of many years.

Tarot for Manifestation

Contents

Tarot for Manifestation

Introduction

The past 35 years or so have seen the tarot grow up. No longer a slave to shallow fortune-telling, the tarot is currently viewed by many to be a helpful symbolic feedback tool that assists us to see our inner and outer options more clearly. The more options of which we are aware, the more empowered we are to make cleaner decisions. These colourful pasteboards are also employed for brainstorming, meditation, creative visualisation, healing, ceremony, journal writing, dance choreography, and more. The only thing that limits the use of tarot is lack of imagination. Instead of a mouthpiece for "fate", the tarot is now a passport to personal responsibility and a royal road to wellness and success.

The focus of this book is manifestation, which is the art and science of making something real. You will use the tarot as a means to clarify your goals and desires and to set up a path to what you want. Five processes or activities are provided. I have worked with every one of them and found each to be effective. Many clients and students have performed these exercises with great success. Indeed, I offer a real-life example at the end of each process so that you can see how it might unfold and how the tarot can trigger fascinating insights and ideas.

Why use tarot as part of your goal-creation process when there are so many good programmes out there that don't employ the cards? Because the cards bring in imagery as well as words. The Deep Self, or whatever you choose to call it, understands the language of symbolism. The tarot is rich with symbols that speak to us on profound levels and thus motivate and inspire us beyond text and speech alone.

Nowhere in Tarot for Manifestation will you see a "recipe list" of card meanings. There are enough excellent tomes out there to provide these (and many abysmal ones). In the examples provided after each exercise you'll read some interpretations and insights based on the way I work with tarot and on the observations of some people who have worked with me. I encourage you to engage with the images and concepts on your cards – interact, write, doodle, meditate, contemplate, tell stories, free associate – so that the ideas you generate are truly your own. Of course, feel free to consult any good tarot texts for additional meanings, but only after you've noted your own perceptions.

I don't advocate the use of any single deck, but rather enjoy many different sets of cards. I believe that it's important to offer the people who come to me an array of tarot decks and let them choose for themselves in order to feel comfortable with the symbols in front of us as we work together. When I use the tarot for myself, I pick a pack of cards depending on my mood or intent, or even based on which deck happens to be nearby. But this approach is my choice. There are other practitioners who prefer to work with one deck and become intimately acquainted with its nuances. That's their choice. Both ways are "correct".

You are invited to either read the entire book cover to cover before performing any of the activities or to just dip in and do one. You can pick sections that appeal to you; there's no need to read or perform them in the order presented. You may find that one chapter works better for certain goals and another exercise does a more efficient job for others. Some activities are geared toward intensive work with one particular goal while others can be used for several at a time. Perhaps you'll do two or more processes for one manifestation project in order to explore different angles and approaches. Maybe the multiple processes will confirm each other. It's possible that you'll resonate with only one of the activities and use it every time you work on making your desires a reality. Explore, experiment, and record your results. However you approach Tarot for Manifestation, I wish you a fabulous life created in your own image!

~ James

Chapter One
PREPARATION FOR MANIFESTATION WITH TAROT

Before embarking on a journey, we consult a map to learn as much as possible about the route and the destination. Before renovating a room, we check to see what we can tear down safely, what needs to stay, what colours will be flattering, what furniture will fit, and whether or not we have the correct tools and skills at hand. This chapter is the preparatory stage for working with tarot for manifestation. It's a toolbox for the process of self-renovation, the "training wheels" that will assist you to ride gracefully through the rest of this book. Those of you with a solid background in tarot or in goal-setting may be able to skip this section, or you might be curious enough to glance at what's offered here. Those of you who are new to, or a little uncertain about, tarot or goal-setting might want to spend some time in this chapter before enjoying the activities in the following chapters.

My Outlook About the Tarot

Bear in mind that this outlook is subjective. It's my current worldview as it is applied to the tarot. As I grow and change, it too will grow and change. You might want to clarify what the tarot is to you, what it's not, what it's for, and what it's not for. This can be in your journal, with a friend, or in a tarot study group. In the meantime, here's where I'm coming from.

Tarot cards are just objects. The deck is simply a tool. Like any tool – computer, hammer, oven, or mathematical formula – the tarot is meant to be used if it works for you and not if you feel it doesn't. Tarot is not a religion or a belief system, but using it can help us to clarify what our beliefs are. The cards carry no power in and of themselves. The power to create, destroy, love, fear, choose, allow, act, or wait lives within us. Tarot cards contain strong universal symbols that assist us to get in touch with those inner powers. How? Ultimately, who knows? I believe that one cannot choose a "wrong" card because every card depicts some aspect of human experience, a point of view that is simply another angle on an issue or question, so whatever card one gets will always be "right".

Our own imagination, creativity, and intuition make the cards relevant to our situations.

All of this said, I believe that there is, in a sense, a spirit of tarot, a "tarot-ness", a sort of archetype of tarot that has taken on life due to repeated use and contemplation of the cards over the past few centuries. How could a tool be employed for so long and not build up a morphic resonance or energy form of some kind?

Basic Tarot Structure

The tarot is deck of 78 symbolic cards which can be divided into two principle sections. One is called the Major Arcana (life's large mysteries), the Trumps, or "big cards". These 22 cards show us the principle universal themes, the what. The other section of the tarot deck is called the Minor Arcana (life's small mysteries) or the suit cards. These 56 pasteboards show us how the big themes show up. The Minors are made up of four suits of 14 cards each – Ace through King. Each suit corresponds with an element (earth, air, water, and fire), season, direction, and aspect of life (physical/tangible, mental/communicative, emotional/relational, and spiritual/energetic).

Variations on imagery, suit names, court card names, and Trump names exist. Each deck's creator has a personal artistic sensibility and a particular philosophy of life which is expressed in the cards s/he publishes. Your deck might come with a book or booklet that explains how the artist came up with the images and why s/he created them as s/he did. To get to know your tarot deck better, it will be helpful for you to sit with your cards for a short time every day and look at them. Deal them off the pack, turn them over slowly, and name them aloud. After a while, you'll know every card at a glance. You can become acquainted with your deck's structure by separating your cards into Majors and Minors. Then deal one card from the Major stack to discover the basic theme and deal one card from the Minor stack to discover how that theme might be playing out or how you can use the theme in your life.

How to Derive Meaning from Your Tarot Cards

A starting point to deriving meaning from your cards is to simply rely on interpretations provided in whatever text accompanies the deck. As you gain more confidence and as you perform the exercises in this book, you will go beyond this. How? Here's a brief list of ideas to help you come up with meaningful information from your cards:

For each card in the deck, set up a page and create a chart on this page. At the top is a space for the card's name. Below this are two columns. The left hand column is devoted to the names of people (authors, friends, teachers) whose resources you consult. The right hand column is for key words and phrases that each of these people provides that you feel have relevance to the card. As you collect ideas in your right hand column, circle or highlight recurring concepts. Group similar ideas together in a space at the bottom of the page. In your own words, distil your circled/highlighted words into meaningful phrases that you can apply to the card. See Appendix A for a chart that you can photocopy and use for all 78 cards.

In a notebook or journal, free associate with objects, symbols, people, actions, colours, shapes, scenes, interaction, animals, plants, and so forth in every card. Spend a good deal of time with each card, jotting down memories, associations, puns, bolt-from-the-blue ideas, emotions, and situations that come to mind as you reflect on each component of the card image. In your notebook, have two of these components dialogue with one another. Then three of them. Write it all down and synthesise what emerges.

Make up a story, fairy tale, or news flash about what's happening in the card picture. Be as imaginative as possible. Retell the story with yourself as the principle character. Any new insights? Write them down.

Prop the card in front of you so that you can see it without discomfort to the neck or eyes. Inhale and exhale slowly and deeply to and from the abdomen a few times to let go of stress. Continue to breathe in this conscious manner, but in your own natural rhythm, taking in the details of the tarot image. What's on the top, middle, bottom? What's on the right, in the centre, on the left? What's in the foreground, middleground, background? Notice as much as possible. Just be with the card. Let your eyes take in the entire scene. Gently close your eyes and reproduce the card in your imagination. Half-open them again to take in a few more details. Close your eyes again and envision the card growing larger in your mind until it's life-size before you. Step over the border of the card and enter the landscape. Use all of your senses – smell, sight, hearing, touch, taste, intuition, and heart – to explore the scene and everything in it. Ask questions of everything and everyone you encounter here (it's Tarot Land, so everything is capable of communication in some form!). Immerse yourself in the feeling or atmosphere of this place. If you wish, carry on an extended conversation – through words, thoughts, symbols, feelings, etc. – with an important figure in your tarot landscape. Let them give you tools, wisdom, and ideas to take back to the mundane world. Merge your body and energy with the figure to know what it feels like to be the card. Then disengage from the figure and thank it. Wander back through your tarot scene and arrive at the edge again. Step back over the border and onto the ground or floor beneath you. See the card shrink down until it's nothing more than a card again. Take a deep breath, stretch, and open your eyes. Record everything in your notebook, recalling as many details as possible. You will now know this card more intimately.

Employ dreamwork techniques used in Jungian/archetypal analysis. I recommend activities in books such as Inner Work (Robert A. Johnson), The Art of Dreaming (Jill Mellick), and the Jungian-Senoi Dreamwork Manual (Strephon Kaplan Williams).

Use techniques from good tarot books like Tarot for Self-Discovery (Nina Lee Braden), Tarot for Your Self (Mary Greer), 21 Ways to Read a Tarot Card (Mary Greer), The Way of Tarot (Alejandro Jodorowsky), Heart of Tarot (Amber K & Azrael Arynn K), Putting the Tarot to Work (Mark McElroy), and Tarot Outside the Box (Valerie Sim).

Read good interpretive books such as Learning the Tarot (Joan Bunning), Choice Centered Tarot (Gail Fairfield), Choice-Centered Relating and the Tarot (Gail Fairfield), The Complete Book of Tarot Reversals (Mary Greer), Seventy-Eight Degrees of Wisdom (Rachel Pollack), Tarot Wisdom (Rachel Pollack), Tarot for Life (Paul Quinn), the Tarot Dictionary and Compendium (Jana Riley), and Pictures from the Heart (Sandra Thomson).

This list of ideas does not exhaust the many ways in which you can gain meaning from a card, but is intended to jumpstart your interpretive capacities.

How to Choose Your Goal(s)

Many of us have so many desires in our heart that we have a hard time figuring out what we'd like to make happen in our lives. It can be frustrating to get stuck when it comes to funneling all of these desires down into concretely expressed goals. Before you perform any of the exercises in this book, it's important to decide what you want to create and to write it down as clearly as possible. Unwritten goals are not goals at all, but merely fantasies. Be realistic if it's a shorter-term objective and more audacious if it's longer-term. Another concern is how specific to make a goal. If it's too vague, there's no focus. If it's too detailed, we experience tunnel vision and think that it can only happen in one form. Be specific enough to be focused, but leave enough room for Life to surprise and delight you. So, what can you do?

The most obvious thing is to ask, "What do I long for?" or "What have I not yet received, experienced, or been that would enrich my life?", then answer that. It might be one or two items or it might be several.

You can sit down with your notebook and brainstorm. Jot down a vast, unedited list of things and qualities to work on obtaining or embodying. Make sure that you have at least 20 items on your list. Can you come up with even more? Walk away from your list for a while, an hour or a couple of days. When your return to your brainstormed list, circle or highlight the goals that would be the most fulfilling or obtainable to you.

You might find it helpful to pick things to accomplish by thinking of the four elements or four suits of the tarot and any qualities or parts of life they represent to you. For example, Pentacles/Earth might inspire you to exercise regularly, renovate your living space, or increase your financial income. Swords/Air could remind you of courses you want to take, travel destinations, or to set clearer communication boundaries. Cups/Water could suggest relating with an intimate partner in a more feeling way, to drink more water, or to develop your intuitive skills. Wands/Fire might inspire you to work on self-esteem, to become a more public figure, or to curb your temper.

Another source of ideas for your goals might be the concepts that dwell in the planets, signs, and houses of your astrological birth chart. Go through a good astrology book to explore these ideas. My favourites include Intuitive Astrology (Elizabeth Rose Campbell), Choice Centered Astrology (Gail Fairfield), and Astrology for Yourself (Demetra George & Douglas Bloch). Use these concepts to help you brainstorm a list of desires on many levels – internal, external, for the next year, for your lifetime, etc.

If you'd prefer to work on one particular target, but have many options from which to choose, ask, "If a magic genie appeared to me right now and could grant me three wishes, what would they be?" Write down these three wishes. Then ask yourself, "If the genie said he was lying the first time, that I could really only have one wish, which one of these three would it be?" Circle or highlight that one wish. It's the single thing to work on manifesting at this time.

Affirmations

Some of the exercises in Tarot for Manifestation ask you to create an affirmation as part of the process. An affirmation is a positive statement that is repeated over and over – verbally, mentally, and/or in writing – in order to reprogramme our beliefs. The result of this is an improvement in whatever area of life for which we are using the affirmation.

Keys to creating and using a helpful affirmation include:

Make it POSITIVE. This is an affirmation, not a negation. Avoid words such as no, not, won't, or isn't as the unconscious tends to ignore these. If you find yourself writing what it is you're not creating or not wanting, ask, "OK, if it's not this, what IS it?" Then write down what the quality or thing IS. For example, if you originally decide on "I am no longer a sad person", change it to something like "I am a joyful person."

Make it PERSONAL. Use words such as I, my, mine, and me. Refer to yourself. The only one you can work on is YOU. You can't use affirmations to change another person, but perhaps by working on yourself, your perception of them will shift. In other words, you can't speak or write an affirmation that says something like "Bernie is becoming a more loving man". Instead, you might say, "Every day, I grow more loving towards all people."

Make it PRESENT. Avoid putting off your evolved quality or delicious payoff to some vague future date. Don't say that "I will" do something or be something. You ARE doing or being it NOW. The idea is to draw the energy of that quality into the present moment. Always ensure that your statement is worded in the NOW. For example, do not say, "I, Margaret, will be prosperous." A better phrase is, "I, Margaret, am a prosperous woman."

Keep it SUCCINCT. Nobody wants to memorise long phrases so keep your affirmation short and to the point. You'll be able to remember it without having to refer to a full page of written material.

Make it ACTIVE. Be liberal with verbs. Instead of saying, "I, James, am happy and rich," I might say, "I, James, savour every moment and gratefully receive life's bounty." Don't go overboard so that it reeks of purple prose, but do make your affirmation interesting.

Use your affirmation for a minimum of 21 days. Research shows that it takes at least 21 days of regular practice to make or break a habit. I've been known to do some affirmations for two or more months! Speak your statement several times in the morning, during the day, and before bed at night. Write it out ten to 20 times every day for at least three weeks. Soak in it!

To get more ideas about affirmations check out books such as Creative Visualization (Shakti Gawain), The Law of Attraction (Michael Losier), and Miracles (Stuart Wilde). These people are masters of the positive statement! Feel free to create affirmations for processes that don't call for it. Just because I don't specify it, doesn't mean that you can't do it.

With this basic information and your written goals in hand, you are now ready to journey through the rest of Tarot for Manifestation.

Chapter Two
THE ADAPT-A-SPREAD METHOD

Let's begin with what is familiar. Many people have favourite pre-existing layouts that they use for tarot consultations. I tend to design a spread to fit the occasion, but once in a while I find that a tried and true pattern is reassuring and right.

In the Adapt-A-Spread Method, you decide on your goal or goals, choose your favourite layout, select cards from your face-up tarot deck, and lay them out consciously in the spread positions. You could think of this as a game of "what if", which the tarot is anyway. Ask yourself, "If I did a regular tarot reading about my goal with this spread, what cards would I like to see turn up in which positions?" Then take those cards out of your pack and place them in your chosen pattern.

I can hear some of you scream, "That's cheating!" No it's not. This book is not about predicting your future, it's about manifesting it.

After you lay out your ideal reading, draw the pattern in your notebook and write in the card names and why you chose each one. Then allow each card to suggest doable, concrete actions for you to perform in order for you to begin to achieve your goal(s).

Look at the spread again. Treat it as if it were a regular reading. Interpret it. Do you learn anything new about your relationship with your desire(s)? If so, what? Are you clearer about how to get what you want? More confused? Have your new insights caused you to refine or reform your goal(s) in any way? How? Do you still want it/them? What deeper things did you learn about yourself? Write down all of this information, including any revisions you might have made to your goal(s).

Leave your spread out on a table. Photocopy, scan, or photograph the layout and keep copies of it around your home, in your work space, on your computer, and on the front cover of your journal or notebook. Make sure that you see it often so that you're reminded of your desires and how to achieve them.

Also perform the actions you came up with. Information and visualisation are useless without action. Do it!

Obviously, you'll use some layouts in the Adapt-A-Spread Method for single goals and others for multiple goals. Well-known spreads that work well for single desires include past-present-future, mind-body-spirit, and the celtic cross. Spreads that can be used for either single or multiple goals include the tree of life and horoscope layouts. Please see Appendix B for the versions of these that I use.

An important issue to address here is what to do if your spread contains positions that are intended to indicate blocks, problems, or challenges. In this instance, you could do one of three things. First, you could change the meaning of the spread position (do I hear more screams?). Second, you could omit it completely (shocking!). Third, you can reflect on what challenges you're realistically willing to deal with in order to reach your target. If you choose the third option, do so consciously. There's no point in laying out a card that, to you, indicates disease or financial difficulty if you're not really willing or able to experience those things.

Here are a couple of interesting variations on the Adapt-A-Spread Method:
After you've laid out your spread, choose one card from your face-down tarot deck to gain extra insight or clarity about the process. What new feedback do you receive from this card? Does this change the way you'll approach your goal(s). If so, how? Does it confirm that you're on the right track? If you gain new insights that cause you to revamp your initial goal(s), feel free to remove any of your original cards and to replace them with one that's more appropriate for the revised version. Your extra clarifying card might be pulled for one of these questions: What unexpected opportunity might change the route to my goal? What unexpected challenge might change the route to my goal? Who or what is my guide on the journey to my goal? What must be in place for this journey to work well for me? What is unacceptable for me to experience on this journey to my goal? What is an alternative way for me to experience the benefits that achieving this goal will bring into my life? What is my true motivation with regard to this goal? Now come up with some of your own clarifying questions.

Let yourself be surprised. Select your cards, as indicated in the original Adapt-A-Spread Method. After laying them out in the pattern, gather up the cards, turn them face-down, and mix them up. Deal them into the pattern as if you're performing a standard reading. Surprise! Is this arrangement better than your original plan? Worse? The same? What interesting slant do you perceive about your goal(s) when you use this variation?

Real-Life Example:
Tara's Horoscope Layout for the Next Two Years

Tara, a 31 year old woman who enjoys camping, art, and ancient cultures, works at a health food store. She decided to work on several goals over a two-year time frame, so we chose the horoscope layout to cover all her bases. She selected the Motherpeace tarot deck, a round Goddess-oriented set of cards with primal story-filled artwork.

Each section of the layout, if it were in a circular astrological chart, would look like a slice of pie. Each "slice of the pie" is called a house and corresponds to a different piece of life. Tara looked over the possibilities of meaning for each house then narrowed them down so they would reflect her specific desires. So, while I'm aware that each house can be many things (astrologers, be kind to me!), the areas of life in parentheses in this particular example are the ones on which the subject chose to focus.

1st House (Sense of personal identity and perhaps a new name). Tara chose the **Ace of Wands** for its sense of being reborn and coming out of her shell. She wants to be in touch with her inner fire and to be able to express it playfully. The action she came up with, based on the Ace of Wands, was to make an appointment with a well-known rebirthing practitioner. She thought it would be a good way to begin her two-year journey of self-creation.

2nd House (Money and other tangible resources). For this, Tara picked the **Son of Discs**. The archer in the picture is focused and on target. She'd like to be fiscally responsible person and to meet all of her financial responsibilities on time. She would also like to be able to contribute what she can to the well-being of others. The Robin Hood-like energy of the central figure suggested that Tara "rob from the rich and give to the poor", so to speak. She decided to tithe 10 percent of her personal income to worthy causes and another 10 percent to her future self so she'd be more secure.

3rd House (Knowledge and local community). The card that best depicted Tara's desire for a group of similar-minded people was the **6 of Swords**, in which six women fly through the air with their swords all pointing towards a common centre. Tara felt that this showed her desire to be part of a study circle or book study group that would expand her mind and her social sphere. Since the people in the card are flying, she came up with the idea to "put up flyers".

4th House (Nurturing home environment or residence). Tara wanted simpler décor and a calm sanctuary where she and her friends could feel nurtured. The **4 of Discs** was her card for this. Its depiction of a woman closing her door in order to spend time in her warm and simple space was perfect. It suggested that Tara slowly go through each room and remove anything that she no longer considered to be useful, attractive, or nurturing, then hold a big yard sale. The patterned discs on the wall prompted her to put her own artwork on her walls, to display her personal creations for enjoyment.

19

5th House (Fun and leisure time). The 9 of Cups was the idea card for Tara to remember to contact her women friends from time to time to hang out, laugh, bitch, and casually catch up. Her doable action was to contact at least nine friends to invite them to her mother's cottage for a weekend of food, drink, merriment, and skinny-dipping.

6th House (Health). Tara felt a need to move her body more, to nourish it through more exercise; however, she abhors gyms. The card that best depicted what she needed was **Temperance**. Its central figure, clad in a grass skirt, is dancing on the beach. It suggested to Tara that she could join a belly-dancing class – healthy and fun!

7th House (Equal relationship with a significant other). Tara chose the **2 of Cups**. This picture of two people toasting each other while diving deeply together reminded Tara that she desired a love partner with whom she could explore rich emotional, psychological, and spiritual depths and with whom she could celebrate mutual accomplishments. The

action that Tara felt this card suggested was to let a healthy love partnership develop naturally over the two-year period (she was drawn to the 2-ness of the card). The image made her feel like intimate connections would work best if they grew organically from her growth-oriented activities.

8th House (Exploring the unseen and magick). For this house, Tara selected the **High Priestess** because she had a desire to know the Dark Goddess and to cultivate an intimacy with Her through ritual and intuitive tools. Suggested actions were to read a book about the Black Madonna that she received on her birthday, get a set of Motherpeace cards, and carry out simple rituals at every dark moon time of the two-year time span.

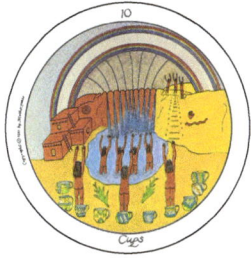

9th House (A cosmology or bigger picture that guides her. Also long-distance travel). The **10 of Cups** was Tara's ideal 9th House card. Its image of a group of women giving thanks in a ceremonial manner reminded her that Nature and awe were what guided her. It also depicted her desire to go on a pilgrimage to honour Nature and Goddess. Tara's doable task as to research facilitators and groups who offer goddess pilgrimages (to Crete? Malta? Greece? Other?) as well as retreat centres located in awe-inspiring natural settings.

10th House (Career path that allows her to shine and be seen). For this piece of her life, Tara chose two cards, the **3 of Wands** and the **9 of Discs**. She longed to be a sacred artist who combines visual art, ceremony, and healing. Her desire was offer these to the public by the end of her two-year manifestation project. Based on these two cards, Tara chose to sketch or paint a minimum of three times per week, especially around the dark moon times when she'd be performing her rituals. There was also a suggestion that her pilgrimage destination(s) could be connected with ancient or tribal art. Caves in France? West Coast First Nations cultures of North America? She'd look into this.

11th House (Group with a vision or greater cause). The **7 of Wands**, with its central woman emitting a flame from her open mouth, represented Tara's desire to have more courage to speak up and speak out, to address injustices to women, queer people, and Nature. For actions, Tara thought that her 3rd House book study circle could focus on writings about social and ecological justice. She could also paint her outrage (and solutions!) and show this art publicly along with written commentary. She could organize a show for several artists, writers, poets, and ritual performers to raise funds for a cause about which she's passionate.

12th House (Depth. The unconscious. The process of transformation and rebirth). For this house, Tara chose **the Moon** for its depiction of a woman wading into deep moonlit waters. The labyrinth in the picture was the perfect metaphor for the journey to her centre that Tara wished to undergo. Tara would pay attention to her dreams, write them down, sketch and paint them, and incorporate them into her dark moon Dark Goddess rituals.

For added insight, Tara pulled a card from the face-down tarot pack. Her intent was to discover what theme, energy, or idea would most likely weave through her two-year manifestation process. The card that came up was Arcanum 15, **the Devil**. This said to us that Tara was creating structures and boundaries wherein she could explore her personal shadow, our culture's shadow, and even the shadow side of deity. It

was also to be a time for Tara to witness what in these shadows has oppressed her, society, and Nature and to offer some way to break those chains.

I offered to do a brief analysis of all the cards that Tara picked. There was only one card from the Swords, but three each of the other suits. This indicated that it would be most fruitful for her to sculpt her life in experiential, relational, and action-based ways instead of simply thinking and talking about it. The combination of the five Majors that she had, including the final insight card, suggested that her goals carried larger themes such as healing oppression by exploring the deep shadow realms through art, dreams, ritual, and a relationship with the Divine Feminine. These insights gave Tara more clarity about her desires, so she modified them a bit and came up with this list of things to create and accomplish:

Begin the two-year journey with a rebirthing session.

Also celebrate the beginning of this journey by enjoying a merry weekend at her mom's cottage with women friends. Remember to have fun with them throughout the two-year time frame – it'll keep her grounded.

Take up belly-dancing.

Give 10 % of her income to groups that support Nature and who offer assistance to the marginalized.

Give 10% her income to herself. Set up a special bank account for this.

Start a social/queer/Nature-centred book study circle.

Create art from her dreams.

Create and perform rituals in honour of the Dark Goddess (Black Madonna?) at each dark moon.

Sketch or paint at least three times every week. Adorn her rituals with these pieces. Hang them in her home. Show them publicly after the two year period is over. Let them be a way for her to speak up and speak out.

Go on two pilgrimages, if possible. One to the caves in the south of France, the other to see West Coast First Nations art and the landscape that inspires it.

Allow an intimate relationship(s) to grow naturally from any of her other activities. Don't force this!

Change her name at the end of the two-year journey. This name will come to her as a result of her explorations and manifestations.

A powerful and courageous couple of years indeed!

Chapter Three
THE BROADCAST METHOD

The Broadcast Method is simple and enjoyable. You use a single card's symbols and concepts as components of a visualisation during which you beam or broadcast your desire to the entire universe. For some reason, I've found that Major Arcana cards work particularly well for this technique. Perhaps it's because they are more archetypal in nature and resonate on a larger scale. Or maybe my own mind just enjoys working with Trumps. Feel free to work with any card(s) that you like.

Begin by selecting a single goal, wish, or desire. Write it down. Go through your tarot deck face up and find a card that best depicts or feels like the essence of your goal. If you know a tarot deck particularly well, you can simply envision or imagine your ideal card in your mind's eye rather than take out a physical card (handy for those moments in the subway or waiting room). At any rate, decide on a card. Write down its name beside or beneath your desire.

Make sure that you won't be disturbed by people, pets, or communication devices. Use the card-entering meditation/journey in Chapter One to go inside of your chosen card's scene. When you feel at home in the tarot landscape, allow yourself to merge with the central person, character, or symbol to become that component of the card.

As the tarot figure, feel yourself solidly planted and grounded in the earth beneath you. Sense that you are larger than life with a consciousness that stretches effortlessly into infinity. Begin to beam out energy or signals. It might radiate from your (i.e. the tarot character's) head, solar plexus, hands, or other body part. Perhaps it will shine from something you're holding or wearing such as a wand, flower, shield, hat, or necklace.

Once the outflow of signals is established, mentally speak as the tarot figure, broadcasting a message to the universe and to any and all interested and helpful parties who can and will assist you to make your desire a reality. If you're alone while doing this, you can even speak your message aloud. Speak spontaneously and with conviction until the broadcast feels complete.

Take a few moments to feel the energy of your broadcast anchor itself in reality. Gently step out of the tarot person or symbol, then exit the card scene. Become yourself, here and now, in your own consciousness and in your own body. Take a deep belly breath, exhale fully, and open your eyes. Declare, "It is so!" or something similar. Get on with your day.

After you practise this method for a while, you should be able to become an appropriate tarot character anywhere and at any time. Perhaps the only chance you'll have to use the Broadcast Method is while you walk to a meeting, listen to a concert, warm up for a soccer match, do the laundry, or shop for groceries. Simply remember the feeling of that other place and time, become the tarot being in your imagination, send out your broadcast, and come back to your everyday awareness.

Real-Life Example: My Own Tarot Broadcast

Here is a moment from my own life when I used the Broadcast Method. One Saturday afternoon, I was scheduled to offer a tarot workshop in a local bookstore. The previous month's event had been poorly attended and I wanted this one to be worth my time and effort. So, before I packed my notes, handouts, and a few tarot decks, I paused to perform the Broadcast Method with the intent to have many appropriate paying attendees. Since I was to be a teacher that day, I decided that the Hierophant, revealer of teachings, would be my best ally.

I took a deep breath and felt myself enter the time and place that is not a time and place. In my mind's eye, I became the Hierophant from the Rider-Waite-Smith tarot deck. On my head was a three-tiered golden crown. My right hand was raised in blessing while my left held a golden staff. The energetic signal began to emanate from all three of these – crown, staff, and hand. As the Hierophant, I mentally sent out an all-call to people who would be interested in tarot in general and my topic in particular. My message included a request to allow me to do what I love to do by being a willing, interesting, and participatory group of people. I concluded by broadcasting the location and time of the event. I thanked everyone and declared, "It is so!" Upon returning to everyday awareness, I felt confident that my message had been received and heard.

When it came time to commence the workshop, I walked into the room, delighted to see four times the number of attendees than I'd had the time before! I mentally thanked my inner Hierophant for his assistance as I proceeded to enjoy my teaching gig.

Chapter Four
HAPPY NEW YEAR MANDALA

This is an activity that I often do close to the end of December or beginning of January to set my goals for the next 12 months and figure out how to make them happen. Mandala is a Sanskrit word that means "magic circle" and refers to a symmetrical pattern used for meditation. In this case, it's a pattern that you create with your goal cards to be a visual reminder of what you choose to manifest in a particular year.

The Happy New Year Mandala is more effective than merely making resolutions because you depict what you've said you'll do or have, then commit to actions that will make these things take place. This is process is simple, but don't do a breezy, sloppy job of it. Set aside time – a day, a weekend, or time each day for several days – to do it well. Remember, this is your ideal life you're creating!

While the Happy New Year Mandala can be done with one tarot deck, two decks are better. The second set of cards can be the same design as the first one or you can use a completely different pack. My own preference is to use two differently imaged decks.

First, write down your goals for the year. Now, turn your tarot deck face up. Pick one goal. Rummage through the cards to find an image that most looks or feels like that particular goal. Set it aside. In your notebook, write the card's name and why you think or feel that it represents your target. Repeat this for every one of your desires, always recording the card and why you chose it. You should now have several images in front of you. This is your Mandala for the year. Meditate on it, create ritual around it, photocopy and post it on your fridge or mirror. It's a visual affirmation, a reminder of what you're aiming for.

Mix up your second tarot deck as thoroughly as possible, holding the intent that the cards you'll pick will suggest constructive actions for you to take. From the face down pack, select one card per goal. Place these in a circle that surrounds your original Mandala, creating an outer layer to it. Use any of the techniques from the "How to Derive Meaning from Your Tarot Cards" section of the first chapter and/or use interpretations that you already know to come up with real activities you can perform that will get you to your goals. Write down all of the suggested actions. Set completion dates for each task, write them in your notebook, and mark them on your calendar. Carry out each action when it is time to do so.

Once you've carried out a suggested action for a particular goal, feel free to remove that action card from the Mandala and replace it with another. Your circular pattern will become a living, changing entity that shifts as you gain fresh insight and create new doable actions.

Some enjoyable things to do to carry this exercise further are:

Do this process on your birthday, your personal New Year.

Make colour copies of your goal cards and actions cards. Stick them on a large piece of cardboard along with pictures and words from magazines, brochures, and newspapers to make a collage of your goals for the year. Add your own sketches and words. Place a photograph of yourself in the centre.

Notice the positive qualities in the cards you've chosen. Turn these into an affirmation to help you programme helpful thoughts. See Chapter One for how to construct an affirmation.

Write a poem about your cards and goals. Recite it aloud often.

Hold a Happy New Year Mandala party with a group of trusted friends. Include food and beverages. Work on your mandalas in a group setting. Make collages together. Read each other's mandala poems. Hold your hands over each other's mandalas to bless them. Toast each other's accomplishments in advance. Half way through the year, you can meet again for a progress party. Make manifestation fun!

Real-Life Example: Gregory's New Year

Last December, I met with Gregory, a 36 year old astrologer and poet, to help him work on six goals for the new year. These were to deepen his relationship with his soul, to go on a retreat or vision quest, to self-publish his first astrology book, to connect with an intelligent and diversity-honouring spiritual community, to double his client base, and to double his financial inflow.

Gregory liked the gentle imagery of the Medicine Woman tarot deck, so he used it to create his mandala. **The Grandmothers** (the Moon in traditional decks) shows a person dreaming deeply and receiving wisdom from an ancient feminine figure. To Gregory, this was someone in deep communion with their soul. To depict a retreat or vision quest, he chose the **3 of Pipes**, in which a lone figure stand atop a high place that overlooks a body of water in the wilderness – perfect! The **10 of Pipes** shows a person drawing or writing at their desk by candlelight. To Gregory, this was the ideal scene of a writer completing a manuscript. For finding an intelligent, diversity-honouring spiritual community, the **7 of Arrows** appealed to Gregory because people from different cultures are facing each other in a circle. Behind them the holy texts of many traditions shine with equal light. The idea of doubling the number of his astrology clients was best represented by the **10 of Stones**, in which a group of people engages in friendly commerce. Gregory's final goal card was Harvest (the Wheel of Fortune in traditional decks), an image of reaping vast bounty for what has been sown. Great for doubling his income! He laid these cards out in a simple circle.

To help Gregory come up with doable actions to achieve each desire, we employed the William Blake Tarot of the Creative Imagination, a pack rich with Blakean art and an inventive spirit. Most of the Majors have been re-titled and the four suits are named Poetry, Music, Science, and Painting. Gregory mixed the cards by smushing them around on the tabletop, then chose six from the face-down "pool".

Man of Poetry

His action step card for deepening his relationship with his soul was the **Man of Poetry**. This made Gregory laugh; he's a poet as well as an astrologer. On a literal level, the card suggested that he devote himself to being more of a man of poetry, to set aside a portion of time every week to read and write poems. The central naked figure walking into darkness suggested that Gregory could enter deeper territory in himself through shadow work in Jungian analysis, dreamwork, and overnight camping trips. He could then record these experiences in the soul-drenched language of poetry.

Woman of Science

The **Woman of Science** was Gregory's key to getting away for a retreat or vision quest. The stellar component of the image, as well as the women looking through a telescope suggested that he check his astrological transits for a time that would best support a soulcentric retreat. It also said to do some research about locations across the continent that resonate with the ideas in his first action card.

XX Liberty

To complete his self-published astrology book, the tarot came up with XX, **Liberty** (Judgement or Aeon in traditional decks). This was a reminder to liberate time every day to get the book work accomplished, not exactly a surprise. Trump # 20 often suggests a rite of passage or a graduation to me, so I offered the idea to Gregory that he remind himself often that writing a book is the natural next step, the next right thing in his astrological work.

The **4 of Poetry's** printed keyword, Harmony, caught Gregory's eye when exploring how to find a spiritual community. He remembered a small group of musicians who provided chants and drumming for spiritual groups, openings of holistic lectures, and such events. The card's central figures walk in nature or a park in a spirit of gratitude or praise. There seemed to be a hint of what theologian Matthew Fox would call deep ecumenism. Gregory and I put these elements together by coming up with an idea for an all-faith Earth Day ceremony in a large local park at which the aforementioned musicians could play and sing. This would afford him the opportunity to meet interesting, conscious people on a spiritual path.

The tarot's suggestion for doubling Gregory's client base was the **3 of Poetry**. There was a sense here of finding three specific target markets, then writing short pieces in publications geared toward them. The open book in the card image said, "Finish the book, then get it out there!" In other words, Gregory's completed astrology book will give him better credibility and visibility, attracting more people to him.

Finally, for Gregory's goal to double his financial inflow, we pulled the **Child of Music**. In this card, the central figure, dressed in a wolfskin, plays a wind instrument as s/he wanders on a mountain path. The concepts of Child (traditionally the Page) plus Music (traditionally Cups) suggested to me that Gregory take more risks in his professional relationships, to extend his services to people about whom he's been hesitant to connect with, to attend more astrology conferences, to take more intuitive and imaginative leaps in his consultations. The wandering aspect of the card character made Gregory think of "taking his show on the road". He could offer workshops in different towns and cities and sell copies of his book to participants. It also reiterated his need to attend more out-of-town events such as symposia and conferences. The central figure's costume made Gregory think of role-play. He

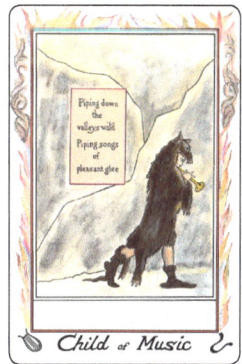

could make his astrological sessions more interactive, inviting clients to role-play what they talk about in order to gain deeper insights. He could even create an "Act Out Your Birth Chart" workshop to offer.

At the time of writing, Gregory has almost completed his astrology book and is contributing a regular column to one of his targets' publications. He's been on one retreat in Northern Ontario and plans to go back. More people are contacting him for consultations. Congratulations, Gregory!

Chapter Five

THE BETWEEN-THE-CARDS METHOD

This is essentially an elaboration on the traditional past-present-possible future(s) layout. However, instead of just declaring, "This happened, that is happening, and the other is likely to happen", you reflect on, depict, and clarify what occurs in the spaces between the cards.

Before you begin the steps below, choose one goal, desire, concern, or topic. Write it down. Now proceed through the numbers in order.

Go through your face-up tarot deck and pick a card for the NOW of the process. How do you feel NOW? Place this card on the surface in front of you and write down your observations as they pertain to your current situation.

From your face-up pack, select a card for a previous stage or milestone in the situation. In other words, what WAS. Place this card slightly to the left of the NOW card. Write about what WAS in the context of the card image. If you know how you got here previously, you can get an idea of patterns, habits, strategies, and circumstances that you'd either like to avoid or recreate, depending on whether or not they were life-affirming. Or an unexpected event may have taken place that triggered your current desire.

What is your ideal scenario with regard to the GOAL? What, for you, would be the ultimate playing out of the situation? Choose a card (or even two cards) from the face-up deck to represent this. Place it to the extreme right of the other cards, leaving some space between it and the first one. Write about this third card. Be as grandiose and imaginative as you wish. Let it be delicious!

Most ultimate goals don't happen overnight, so pick a card from the face-up pack to depict how you can see the desire or situation playing out in the NEAR FUTURE. What's the next milestone? Project yourself and the situation a little bit ahead of the present. Place the card for this between the first and third cards. Write about it.

Now it's time to define the energy and path of the space between the WAS card and the NOW card. What transpired between the last milestone and the present? Write about it. How did it feel? What did you do? Pick a face-up card to depict this path. Place it between and above Cards 2 and 1. What might you do the same? What might you do differently? Write about all of these things too.

Now spend some time with the space between NOW and the NEAR FUTURE. How would you like to feel on your way there? The feeling is important; it will be your motivator, your ideal energetic state between the present and what's to come. Choose a card, face up, to represent these feelings. Place it between and above Cards 1 and 4.

Use your final card as an inspiration for doable, concrete actions to perform. Brainstorm, free-associate, make lists, don't edit, be creative. Only after you've generated a substantial cluster of ideas should you narrow them down. Choose one to four steps to take between now and a specific date (did Card 6 suggest any time frame to you?) and commit yourself to them. Do them!

Your final pattern of cards should look like this:

$$5 \quad 6$$
$$2 \quad 1 \quad 4 \quad 3$$

By consciously defining and depicting the energies of the gaps between the cards, you've made a blueprint to get what you want.

Real-Life Example: Aldeth's Healing Practice

Aldeth is a 29 year old massage therapist, accupuncturist, and reiki practitioner with a busy one-on-one practice. She wanted to integrate her already existing healing work with a burgeoning interest in the Divine Feminine and self-created ceremony without alienating anyone. Aldeth's desire to work with groups was growing. She had been reading books by Starhawk, Merlin Stone, Sedonia Cahill, and others for about a year and a half by the time of our meeting. She also wanted to move to the Canadian West Coast and transfer her practice there.

For this activity, Aldeth picked cards from the Daughters of the Moon Tarot, a round-shaped, feminist, goddess-honouring set of cards. Our session felt like a council of three creative spirits – hers, mine, and the tarot's.

First, Aldeth chose a card to represent her healing practice in the present. She settled on the **One of Pentacles** because the central figure looks healthy, balanced, competent, comfortable with who she is, excellent at working with energy, and practising what she preaches in her own life. This character seemed, to Aldeth, to be a master of her craft and a clear vessel for the Life Force.

Next, she chose a card to depict a pivotal event in the recent past that affected her practice. The card was the **Nine of Flames**. This picture of a woman pulling her caravan down the road reminded her of a decision to leave a yoga studio where she rented space for a couple of years. The administrators there started limiting her schedule and she got tired of paying them. To Aldeth, the woman in the card looked strong, confident, and ready to break off on her own. It represented her willingness to leave one phase behind and enter the next with purpose and determination.

Then I asked Aldeth to find a card that most looked and felt like her ideal integration of her healing modalities with Goddess spirituality and ceremony. She selected two cards, the **Six of Cups** and **Celebration** (roughly equivalent to the traditional Judgement card). The landscapes were a perfect bland of beach and mountain, Aldeth's West Coast dream. The group vibe of each images suggested retreats – women's getaways during which they could do ritual, offer each other massage and energy healing, pray, meditate, and celebrate in community while reconnecting with the power of Nature, the moon, the earth, their bodies.

Knowing that most ideal goals don't fall into our laps overnight, I suggested that Aldeth choose a card for how she envisions her practice unfolding over the next year or so, the near and doable future. Her choice was the **Ten of Cups**, a picture of a small group of woman holding hands under a waterfall. To her, it looked like a goddess grotto and suggested that she could place a small altar in the form of a water fountain in her healing room. The Ten of Cups also represented an intimate group celebrating the Feminine together in the comfort of familiar space – perhaps her house here in Toronto – in simple, grassroots ways.

So far, we had clarified her present, a pivotal moment in her past, the near future, and her ultimate goal. Between these cards lay spaces pulsing with feeling and action calling out to be identified. I asked Aldeth to think about leaving the yoga studio and then about the centred, professional person she is now, then choose a card to reflect how the journey from one to the other felt to her. The Four of Blades looked like a woman who is objective, balanced, and in charge of her own decisions. Aldeth saw a person weighing options without interference. Two remaining swords under the seat reminded Aldeth of extra resources she had during that time in the form of tools, contacts, and ideas she kept "up her sleeve".

The final card that Aldeth chose was for her path from the now (One of Pentacles) to the next forseeable phase (Ten of Cups) and how that should feel. It was important to know the qualities she wanted to feel within herself before knowing what the actions would be. She selected the Ten of Pentacles for its sense of community, love, nourishment, and informality. Aldeth wanted the journey to be relaxed, loving, and community-oriented.

For the "how", the concrete steps, we used the picture on Aldeth's final card to brainstorm what she could do to embody those feelings. The image suggested a few great ideas. First, a pot-luck goddess picnic where people could get to know her and each other in friendly atmosphere. Second, an informal open house in her professional space. Aldeth would use these two events to promote a women's wellness retreat to be offered that Autumn, suggested by the depiction of harvested fruit in the card.

Aldeth aimed to get 10 attendees at her first ever retreat. Because of the two free community-building events beforehand, she ended up with 22 people! This bodes well for building a West Coast centre for healing and group events.

Chapter 6
THE CLEARING AND AFFIRMING METHOD

This manifestation exercise is very powerful! It's a blend of ideas from Shakti Gawain's Creative Visualization, aspects of Mary Greer's Breakthrough Process in Tarot Mirrors, and some things of my own. When you experience the Clearing and Affirming Method, you will uncover negative beliefs, blocks, and stumbling points, both conscious and unconscious, that get in the way of your success. Then, you will be able to clearly and confidently accentuate the positive and perform your goal-building tasks with joy and enthusiasm.

 Name the quality, event, thing, identity, or whatever it is you choose to create. Write down your goal. It can be something in your inner life or in your outer world.

Go through your face-up tarot deck and consciously choose a card that, to you, most looks or feels like your goal. You might end up with a small pile of cards to begin with, but narrow your decision down to one card. A good way to figure this out is to ask yourself as you look at each card, "Is this the final result or is this just a step toward the final result?" If the card image is only a stepping stone, put it back into the deck. You want an image of your actualized desire. Write down the name of this card.

Use the card's helpful, evolved, constructive, positive qualities to create an affirmation related to your chosen goal. Make your affirmation succinct, positive, personal, and in the present tense. Also include your name in it. Play with the word order until it "clicks" in your psyche and body, until it feels right. Write down your affirmation. Here are some examples:

I, David, grow in health, wealth, and wisdom every day.

I, Betty, am a vehicle for Universal Creativity.

I, Angelo, open my body and soul to healing and positive change.

I, Miriam, trust that our world is a safe and loving place.

Write down two more versions of your affirmation, one in the second person ("you") and the other in the third person ("he/she"). In other words, you will end up with three versions of your affirmation. Using one of the examples from above, these three versions would be:

I, Angelo, open my body and soul to healing and positive change.

Angelo, you open your body and soul to healing and positive change.

Angelo opens his body and soul to healing and positive change.

For the next step, have two blank pages in front of you. These can be two pages of an opened notebook or simply two sheets of paper on the table. Also have a pen or pencil at hand. Designate the left-hand page for your affirmation. Designate the right-hand page for Little Nasties (you'll see what I mean in a moment).

On the left-hand page, right out your affirmation in its three forms – first-, second-, and third-person – 10 to 20 times at a sitting, aware of each word as you write it. It's important to be intimately connected through pen, fingers, hand, and arm to the nuances and motions of what you write, so don't do this on a keyboard. Write it in longhand or print it, but do it by hand. You can always type up a summary afterwards, if you wish. As you write your affirmation in its three forms 10 to 20 times, notice any negative, unevolved, sabotaging thoughts, ideas, or feelings that arise. Whenever this happens, jot it down on the right-hand page. Even if a Little Nasty seems trivial, silly, or small, write it down. Continue to write your affirmation in its three forms on the left-hand page until you're finished.

When you finish writing your affirmations and other thoughts, look at your Little Nasties page. Read what your mind generated that sabotages your efforts to get to your goal. Go through your tarot pack face up and find one card for each of these negative statements. Place these cards in a row in front of you and write down their names.

Write a story about your row of Little Nasties cards. It can be a fairy tale, a short story, a movie synopsis, or whatever you want to create. Be imaginative and use the pictures to inspire your tale. If writing it seems like a huge task at this point, speak it into a recording device and transcribe it later. Now tell your story again with YOU as the main character. What does this narrative tell you about what obstructs the path that leads to your desired outcome? What destructive beliefs or thoughts lurk beneath the surface? Write down your insights.

Going through your face-up tarot deck again, look for cards whose helpful qualities look as though they cancel out your problematic cards. Place your positive, constructive images on top of the negative ones. Block them out! You should now be able to see only helpful pictures before you. For each helpful card, create and write an affirmation in all three forms, just like you did with your original goal card. Write or speak a story about your positive cards. Once again, it can be any type of narrative that you wish to weave. Retell this happy story with YOU as the main character. What does this new story suggest about attaining your desire? What's the path to get there?

Based on your original goal card and any or all of your positive helper cards, create a series of doable, concrete actions. Commit, in writing, to performing these actions within specific time frames. For example,

I, James, will send a donation to the Calling the Circle Foundation before December the First of this year.

Or

I, Miriam, will enroll in a self-assertiveness training class tomorrow afternoon.

Write and speak all three forms of your affirmation every day for a minimum of 21 days, the minimum time frame it takes to make or break a habit. Write it out at least 10 to 20 times every day. Have a Little Nasties page ready, just in case more unsavoury thoughts or feelings come to the surface during affirmation time. The more you do this process, the less often the Little Nasties will show up. Eventually, a moment will arise when they don't show up at all!

Remember to commit to at least one tangible action per week. Some people have even done one every day. Base these on your cards, your affirmation, and the opportunities that open up to you as you journey closer to your goal. Whatever you do, enjoy the process one day at a time.

Ideas to enhance the Clearing and Affirming Method include:

Write the words, "I am not this" at the top of your Little Nasties page, then burn it and scatter the ashes.

Do this exercise in a sacred ceremonial context. Light candles and/or incense. Invite the Sacred to be present with you. Drum, rattle, or chant before and after your Clearing and Affirming session. Bless your affirmation pages with essential oils.

Lay out your goal card and our positive helper cards on an altar where you can speak your affirmations as prayers.

Photocopy your goal card and your positive helper cards. Stick the images around your home, in your car, in your office, on your wallet, etc. so that you are constantly reminded that your desire is yours to attain.

Real-Life Example: True Love for Patricia

Patricia is a 55 year old floral arranger who enjoys tai chi, gardening, and learning about the medicinal properties of plants. Her charming Victorian home is nestled among various herbs, shrubs, and flowers. When she did the Clearing and Affirming Method with me, Patricia's goal was to be an equal partner in a healthy, loving, mutually satisfying intimate relationship with a long-term male partner. Her marriage, which ended 28 years before, was unpleasant and, in her words, an example of how not to relate. At the time of our meeting, she had done a lot of thinking and therapy around romantic love and felt ready to be intimate with another person.

The tarot deck she chose to work with was the Shining Tribe Tarot, which contains images that reflect ancient shamanic ways of being from many cultures and traditions. It suit names – Trees, Rivers, Birds, and Stones – are from Nature rather than human-made objects.

The three forms of affirmation that Patricia formulated were:

I, Patricia, open my heart, home, and life to my beloved equal.

Patricia, you open your heart, home, and life to your beloved equal.

Patricia opens her heart, home, and life to her beloved equal.

As she wrote these in her journal, the Little Nasty thoughts that came to her were:

I'm too old for this.

Nobody wants "used goods".

My peaceful home life will be disrupted.

The dating scene is dog-eat-dog; they'll eat me alive!

Patricia depicted the first negative thought with **Justice** because the central figure seemed old and prune-like and locked away from the world. The **9 of Trees** was her choice for "used goods". In it, she saw a woman lamenting the creaks and cracks in her body. The third Little Nasty was represented by the **10 of Birds** – busy, frantic, and overwhelming. The final thought, the "dog-eat-dog" dating scene, was depicted by the **5 of Bird**s; the supine figure appeared vulnerable, exposed, ready to be consumed by vultures.

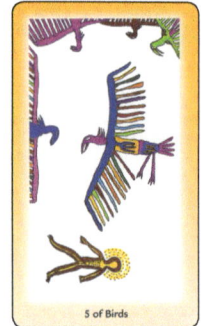

Based on these four cards, Patricia made up a story:

Once upon a time, a withered old woman lived in a cave. She had stayed there for many years because it felt safe to do so. One day, the woman heard a strange bird-like squawk, so she ventured out of the cave and down the path to investigate. It was hot and bright outside, so the old woman sought shelter under a mysterious tree. As she knelt there, the tree lost all foliage, and she heard and felt the shriek of many large, scary birds coming closer. The old woman trembled and covered her eyes, so awesomely frightening was this spectacle. It proved to be too much for her, so she passed out. While she was unconscious, the birds swooped in and devoured her body, piece by piece, until only the vague glimmer of her spirit remained, and that barely. The End.

When I asked Patricia to summarise this story, she told me that it was the tale of a woman who took a great risk only to be violated by doing so. When asked how this synopsis related to her own life experience, she responded by telling me that she married in her early 20s to get out of her parents' home. Very soon, she discovered that her husband was verbally and sexually abusive as well as a compulsive liar. It felt as though he just about sucked every last ounce of life from her. I reminded her that she had the courage to leave the marriage and that she had done a lot of good inner work around that issue.

To block out the negative images, Patricia went through the Shining Tribe deck and came up with four positive helpers. The first one, **Knower of Rivers**, shows a figure coming out of a cave. To Patricia, the person seemed happy, courageous, and eager to share the treasures she found in the depths. In the **2 of Trees**, she saw a woman who basks in the glory and warmth of sunlight

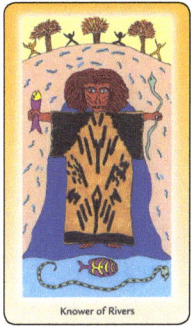

and who gratefully celebrates life. The **Place of Rivers** reminded Patricia that she can take time out for meditation and reflection no matter what is going on around her, that it's OK for her to have "me time". Her fourth helper card was the **Knower of Stones**. The central figure's hair sticks straight on end and she is surrounded by glyphs and symbols. Patricia saw this as a scarecrow who can bristle up to frighten the vultures away. She said that it was a great representation of the power to say "NO!" with a mighty roar and from a place of authentic power and groundedness.

Patricia's affirmations based on her helper cards were as follows. For brevity's sake, I'm only providing you with the first-person form of each:

It's OK for me, Patricia, to share my gifts with the world.

I, Patricia, celebrate the goodness of life.

I, Patricia, am a temple of peace.

In every situation, I, Patricia, respond with strength and authentic power.

Here is her new story, based on the four positive cards:

Once upon a time, a woman emerged from a cavern bearing special gifts that she had found in the depths. She was happy to be in the fresh air and light, so she chanted songs of praise and gratitude to the Source of Life, then offered her special gifts to the community. People took only what they needed and the woman enjoyed her interactions with them. She balanced this social sharing with times of meditative solitude. The community respected these moments by leaving her alone. Because the woman balanced community life with alone time, her body and mind were alive, strong, clear, and alert. Cues and signs from the world around her registered in her body, so she was in tune with opportunities and when to pursue them. Thus she succeeded in all she undertook. The End.

From this story, we created a list of concrete actions for Patricia to consider: Emerge from the cave & community sharing ◊ Attend more social functions. E.g. open houses at the dojo, join or start a gardening club, go to singles evenings at the museum.

Offering/Sharing her gifts ◊ She's good at tai chi and plant. Put up an ad to teach a weekly tai chi class. Give herb identification walks in the large park near her home.

Balance community & private time ◊ Reduce work hours at the flower shop to four days a week. One of the other employees wants an extra day of work anyhow.

Aware of cues & signs resonating in body & mind ◊ When interacting with any of the groups, classes, etc. mentioned above, be conscious of subtle (and not so subtle!) cues that someone is interested in her. Be aware of their body language, words they use, hints they drop, tone of voice, etc. However, don't obsess about being aware of cues. Be in my own power!

As Summer unfolded, Patricia took action based on ideas from her Clearing and Affirming session. The following September, while conducting one of her new herbal walks, she kept feeling as though someone was looking at her. Remembering her pledge to be aware of such cues, she discovered that one of her attendees, Frank, was paying a lot of attention to her. At the end of the walk, Frank invited Patricia to join him for coffee and a chat, so she did, remembering to make that decision from a strong place in herself. At the time of writing, Patricia and Frank (another avid gardener) have been dating for several months.

AFTERWORD

Thank you for joining me on this journey of Tarot for Manifestation! I've enjoyed sharing these activities. It's my sincere wish that they will enhance your life and growth as much as they've enhanced mine.

By now, the benefits of combining tarot with goal-setting are apparent. You're able to see, feel, and try on your desires by laying them on the table before committing to them. You can assess ahead of time whether or not a goal is right for you, saving you valuable time, effort, and perhaps money. Your sense of personal power is stronger because you're making conscious choices about what you want and don't want and about your emotional response to those options.

Look for a moment at the Gaian Tarot's Nine of Water image on the cover of this book. The central character is living what this book is all about. She has entered sacred space and has opened herself to the Creative Energy of All That Is. By working with these processes, so have you! The joy she feels is palpable. You too have created joy in your life! Her state of awe and liberation is the great goal to which we all aspire in the realization of our smaller goals.

I hope that as you've read and worked through these chapters you've learned that the tarot can be for so much more than readings. Your next step is to make these processes your own. Adapt them in any way that works for you. Jot ideas in the margins. Create your own manifestation activities. I'd love to hear what you come up with!

Appendix A
CARD MEANINGS SYNOPSIS CHART

(permission is granted by the author for you to photocopy this page for personal study purposes)

Name of the Card:

Authors' Names   Authors' Key Words and Phrases for This Card

My Personal Summary of This Card's Meanings:

Appendix B

WELL-KNOWN TAROT LAYOUTS

This section contains layouts/spreads that are pretty standard; however, the names that I give to their positions may vary from what you've seen in other texts. Feel free to use any version(s) that you find most helpful for your exploration or manifestation process.

Three-Card Layouts

1	2	3

| Body | Mind | Spirit |
| Me | Other | Our Relationship |

| Situation | Advice | Result |
| Situation | To Leave | To Enter |

The Celtic Cross

There are many variations on this classic layout. I became dissatisfied with most of them, so I created my own wording for each position.

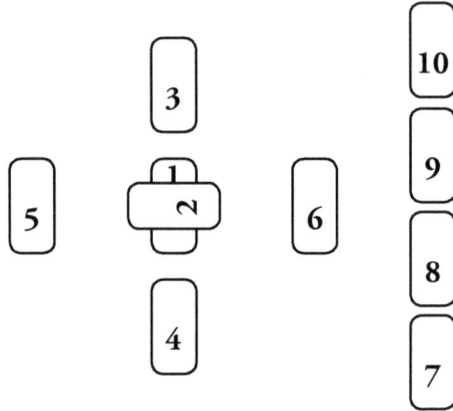

1. One polarity in this situation/process/journey/choice (or One polarity in my life right now).

2. The other polarity in this situation/process/journey/choice (or The other polarity in my life right now).

3. Factors that are conscious, known, or obvious.

4. Factors that are unconscious, unknown, or subtle.

5. What is appropriate for me to leave behind.

6. What is appropriate for me to move towards.

7. All that is "me" in this situation/process/journey/choice (or All that is "me" at this time).

8. All that is "not me" in this situation/process/journey/choice (or All that is "not me" at this time). The other(s) or the environment.

9. Hopes, fears, and the deeper, larger lesson(s) for me to learn around this situation/process/journey/choice (or at this time).

10. What will most likely happen [by such-and-such time] as a result of this situation/process/journey/choice.

The Horoscope Layout

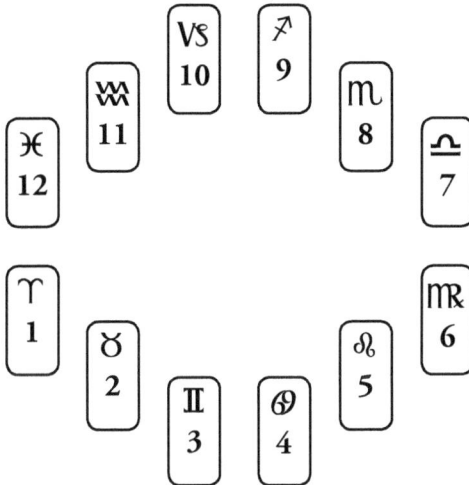

1. My identity, sense of self, who I am as an individual, first impression on others, persona, name.

2. How I pay my own way, my money, my possessions, stable self-resourcefulness, resources, self-esteem.

3. My personal voice or vision, speech, modes of communication, local community, learning and teaching, short journeys.

4. Sense of home, self-care from the roots up, emotional security, mother, residence, nurturance.

5. My sense of play, pleasure, leisure, children, inner child, creativity.

6. My day-to-day work, contribution to the community, service to others, health, nutrition, my routine experiences.

7. Partnership, significant other(s), companionship, peers, contracts, small group experiences.

8. Exploring the unseen, identification with something greater than myself, the occult, sexual expression, other people's resources, death.

9. Worldly wisdom, a cosmology that guides me, philosophy, my sense of the bigger picture, higher education, long-distance travel.

10. My public reputation, status, my vocation, father, authority, a place in the world that is mine where I can shine and be seen.

11. Long-term goals, networking with others, group associations, greater vision, social reform, larger endeavours.

12. Answering the spirit call, connection with the mystical world, infinite imagination, psychic experiences, the unconscious, the process of transformation and rebirth.

Tree of Life Layout

I've rarely, if ever, come across a version of this layout that made any sense to the average person who wants practical guidance without wading through volumes of esoteric texts. This version of the Tree of Life spread is my attempt to keep it simple.

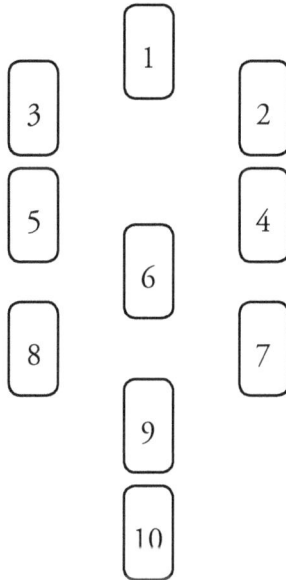

```
              ┌───┐
              │ 1 │
    ┌───┐     └───┘     ┌───┐
    │ 3 │               │ 2 │
    └───┘               └───┘
    ┌───┐               ┌───┐
    │ 5 │               │ 4 │
    └───┘     ┌───┐     └───┘
              │ 6 │
              └───┘
    ┌───┐               ┌───┐
    │ 8 │               │ 7 │
    └───┘               └───┘
              ┌───┐
              │ 9 │
              └───┘
              ┌───┐
              │10 │
              └───┘
```

1. What caused this project/process to come into being?

2. What actions and resources are mine to offer to this project/process?

3. What actions and resources would it be appropriate for me to receive from others in this project/process?

4. What generous compromises am I willing and able to make with regard to this project/process? What is negotiable?

5. What am I absolutely unwilling and unable to compromise with regard to this project/process? What is non-negotiable?

6. What is at the heart or core of this project/process?

7. What are my true feelings about this project/process?

8. What known, conscious, transparent information is most helpful to me with regard to this project/process?

9. What, so far, is unknown, unconscious, or hidden that would be helpful for me to be aware of with regard to this project/process?

10. What is the best venue, setting, or home for this project/process?

BIBLIOGRAPHY

Nina Lee Braden. <u>Tarot for Self-Discovery</u>. Llewellyn Publications.

Joan Bunning. <u>Learning the Tarot</u>: A Tarot Book for Beginners. Red Wheel / Weiser.

Elizabeth Rose Campbell. <u>Intuitive Astrology: Follow Your Best Instincts to Become Who You Always Intended to Be</u>. Ballantine Books.

Laura Day. <u>The Circle: How the Power of a Single Wish Can Change Your Life</u>. Jeremy P. Tarcher.

Gail Fairfield. <u>Choice Centered Astrology</u>. Weiser Books.

Gail Fairfield. <u>Choice Centered Relating and the Tarot</u>. Weiser Books.

Gail Fairfield. <u>Choice Centered Tarot</u>. Newcastle Publishing Company.

Shakti Gawain. <u>Creative Visualization: Use the Power of Your Imagination to Create What You Want in Your Life</u>. New World Books.

Demetra George & Douglas Bloch. <u>Astrology for Yourself</u>. Ibis Press.

Mary K. Greer. <u>The Complete Book of Tarot Reversals</u>. Llewellyn Publications.

Mary K. Greer. <u>Tarot For Your Self: A Workbook for Personal Transformation. (2nd edition)</u>. New Page Books.

Mary K. Greer. <u>21 Ways to Read a Tarot Card</u>. Llewellyn Publications.

Robert A. Johnson. <u>Inner Work: Using Dreams and Creative Imagination for Personal Growth and Integration</u>. HarperSanFrancisco.

Amber K & Azrael Arynn K. <u>Heart of Tarot: An Intuitive Approach</u>. Llewellyn Publications.

Michael Losier. <u>Law of Attraction</u>. Devorss & Co.

Mark McElroy. <u>Putting the Tarot to Work</u>. Llewellyn Publications.

Mark McElroy. <u>Taking the Tarot to Heart</u>. Llewellyn Publications.

Jill Mellick. <u>The Art of Dreaming: A Creativity Toolbox for Dreamwork.</u> <u>Conari Press</u>.

Rachel Pollack. <u>Seventy-Eight Degrees of Wisdom: A Book of Tarot (2nd</u> <u>edition)</u>. Thorsons Publishers.

Rachel Pollack. <u>Tarot Wisdom: Spiritual Teachings and Deeper Meanings</u>. Llewellyn Publications.

Jane Roberts <u>(Channeling Seth). The Nature of Personal Reality (reprint</u> <u>edition)</u>. Amber-Allen Publishing.

Jana Riley. <u>Tarot Dictionary and Compendium</u>. Weiser Books.

Valerie Sim. <u>Tarot Outside the Box</u>. Llewellyn Publications.

Sandra A. Thomson. <u>Pictures from the Heart</u>: A Tarot Dictionary. St. Martin's Press.

James Wanless. <u>Voyager Tarot: Way of the Great Oracle</u>. Fair Winds Press.

Stuart Wilde. <u>Miracles</u>. Hay House.

Strephon Kaplan Williams. <u>The Jungian-Senoi Dreamwork Manual</u>. Journey Press.

ABOUT THE AUTHOR

JAMES WELLS is a Toronto-based motivational listener, consultant, teacher, and facilitator who is dedicated to merging soul and strategy. From childhood, he has been curious about what makes people and the Universe tick. Through tools and processes such as circle methodology, tarot, reiki, and journal writing, James and his clients and students are invited into the presence of their creativity, resourcefulness, and wholeness. Whether at home or abroad, whether in personal sessions or in workshop settings, he provides an experience of council mind. In his "me time", James enjoys reading, writing, music, walking, close friends, and good food.

James would love to receive stories about your journey with this book. You can also contact him to set up personal consultations (by telephone or in person) and to arrange for workshops, retreats, or lectures in your area.

circleways@yahoo.ca
http://jameswells.wordpress.com/

Tarot for Manifestation

www.ingramcontent.com/pod-product-compliance
Lightning Source LLC
Chambersburg PA
CBHW042107110426

42742CB00033BA/22